20 SHORT WALKS
near CALAIS, France

Twenty walks within easy reach of
Calais for drivers, families and dogs

Lezli Rees

Laughing Dog Media
Warwickshire, UK

First published in May 2014 by Laughing Dog Media, The Studio, 205 High Street, Henley-in-Arden, Warwickshire B95 5BA.

ISBN 978-0-9927197-0-8 © 2014 Lezli Rees.

The contents of this book are believed correct at the time of printing. Nevertheless neither the author nor the publisher can be held responsible for any errors or omissions or for changes in the details given in the book, or for the consequences of any reliance on the information it provides. This does not affect your statutory rights. We have tried to ensure accuracy in the book but things do change and we would be grateful if readers would advise us of any inaccuracies they may encounter at info@drivingwithdogs.co.uk

We have taken care to ensure that these walks are safe. The author or publisher cannot accept responsibility for any injuries caused to readers whilst following these walks.

British Library Cataloguing in Publication Data. A catalogue record for this book is available from the British Library.

Illustrations by Karen Blake
Map drawn by the author

About the Author

Lezli Rees has lived with dogs all her life and is a keen walker and rambler. Together with her husband, David Rees and their rescue dog, Jem, the couple have created the UK's best resource of tried and tested dog walks, and own the popular Driving with Dogs website.

When not exploring hidden byways of the countryside, Lezli teaches English at a university in the Midlands.

Contents

Walks   **Page**

Where the walls are

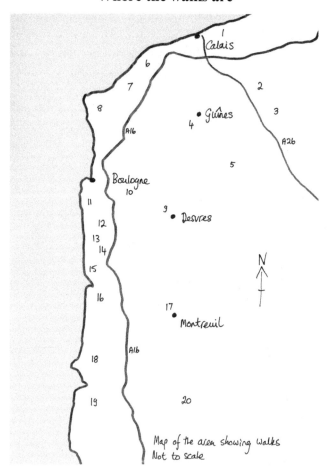

Map of the area showing walks
Not to scale

Introduction

Researching this book has been a delight. Not only has it let me explore a small part of France that was completely new but also to discover the warmth and genuine hospitality of the residents of the Pas de Calais and the Opal Coast.

Complete strangers were keen to point out the best walking places in the enormous forests of Northern France. Dog-walkers provided a wealth of information about dog etiquette and excellent advice concerning when a visit to the vet is considered necessary or not after insect bites. North France presents no greater risk to pets than the UK but it was reassuring to learn that vet treatment is considerably cheaper in France and also that many vets speak extremely good English.

Even in the busy school holiday season in July and August, families may be surprised by the spontaneous warm welcomes and curiosity of rural folk aroused by the appearance of visitors on foot. We were charmed to be invited to join family picnics, to be taken to meet prized farm animals, and to receive expert tuition in foraging for berries and edible mushrooms from locals whose laughter and enthusiasm made us fall in love with the Pas de Calais.

The walks have been fully tried and tested, but please bear in mind that coastal paths in particular are subject to re-shaping by the strong tides and currents of the sea. You may find that slight changes to the quality of the paths will take place from year to year, but the overall route will remain unchanged.

I hope the walks in this book will serve as an introduction to the Pas de Calais and the astonishing beaches of the Opal Coast and that you may be inspired to spend more time exploring the region in the future.

I would like to thank the many anonymous dog-walkers who shared their thoughts on a vast range of canine topics, and the helpful staff of the region's Tourist Information Offices – especially those in Berck and Montruiel. Special thanks are due to David Rees who has walked all the routes with me and also undertook the driving. Our rescue collie, Jem, with his unstoppable energy and a truly omnivorous approach to food made the research trips fabulously worthwhile.

Lezli Rees
May 2014

Éperlecques Forest

About the walks

More and more of us are now using the Pet Passport scheme to take our family pets across the Channel for day trips or holidays in France. This handy guide shows you where to find really good walk places for you and your pet within easy driving distance of Calais, and to discover some of the extraordinary, and dog-friendly, visitor attractions of this much overlooked part of France.

Each walk has written directions to the start point, and the GPS co-ordinates; plus detailed information for campervan drivers. The nearest fuel stations, supermarkets, tourist information offices, vets and cafés to each walk are given, together with useful local information.

The walks are all within an easy drive from Calais. Several walks are within just a few minutes' drive of the Eurostar terminus and Calais ferry port. These are ideal for a leg stretch before or after a channel crossing.

Other walks lie in hidden pockets of the Pas de Calais and enable you to combine a great walk with a fascinating place to visit. For example, you could visit the open-air museum of Éperlecques – with its dramatic story of London-bound rockets during World War 2 – and also take a stroll in the surrounding national forest. Éperlecques Forest is a safe spot for kids and dogs to dash around without restraint.

The beaches of the Opal Coast offer mile after mile of golden sand, and can't be beaten for swimming, beach games and friendly cafés and bistros right on the sea front. I've selected beaches where dogs are given a fantastic welcome, and there's plenty for all the family to do.

Several walks are close to historic sites, from a harbour where King Henry III created chaos trying to load elephants onto a small boat, to the site of the Battle of Crécy, and poignant reminders of World Wars One and Two.

You could also visit the town that inspired Les Misérables, or the exact spot where Blériot touched down after successfully making the first airborne crossing of the English Channel.

All the walks in the book are suitable for children, leisure walkers and dogs, and are at an 'easy' grade. The selected walk places have been chosen to enable you to enjoy a walk of the length and time that suits you, without the need to buy maps or specialist walking gear. If you grow to love the area and want to explore more, the IGN 'green' map series 101, 103 and 107 are recommended.

Walking in France

Walkers have many paths to explore throughout the forests, coast and fields of the Pas de Calais and the Opal Coast. A basic understanding of the French waymarker system will help you walk with extra confidence, although all the walks in this book can be easily managed without any special navigation skills.

Long distance trails, such as the coastal path around much of the north coast, are marked with UK-style wooden waymarker posts with a red and white painted stripe. For example, the route number of the coastal path that winds along much of the Northern coastline is GR120. This number, together with the name of the nearest village or town, will be written onto the wooden post which works just like a signpost. All you need do is to follow the direction pointed out and you'll reach your destination.

In the countryside, quiet lanes (for horse-riders, cyclists, farm vehicles, walkers and the occasional car) are indicated with red and white bollards at either end and are roughly the equivalent of a Bridleway.

Footpaths are indicated by coloured symbols stencilled onto trees or other upright structures at eye level.

Dog Etiquette

Without a language barrier, dogs from either side of the Channel will interact normally with each other. Any difficulties will often arise from the different dog training and socialisation habits of their accompanying people.

Our collie, Jem, proved to be a great conversation opener with local dog walkers and the following observations are based on dog chats with French dog walkers we met on the walks, vets and members of French internet dog forums who kindly shared their views and experiences of dog walking. Obviously, each dog and owner is different and the tips that follow are necessarily generalised.

When walking in the forests most dogs will be off-lead. However, when another dog is spotted you can expect to see the owner put their dog on the lead immediately to avoid an off-lead encounter. If you see this happening, etiquette is to put your dog on the lead too. One reason for this is that dogs in France tend not to be socialised through training classes, and are consequently unsure of the canine play rules. What

British dog owners might regard as boisterous play may be seen as very frightening by a French dog walker.

Once dogs are safely on lead, do expect to be engaged in a doggie conversation – particularly if your pooch is a stylish breed.

The exception to this on-lead rule is working dogs. When you encounter a country hunter, often clad in ancient tweeds and with a gun over his arm, his Brittany spaniel or pointer will be off-lead and working. Any attempt by your dog to say 'bonjour' will meet with a dignified indifference from the dog and an icy Gallic silence from the hunter. Best to put Fido on lead in this situation.

Dogs are generally welcomed in cafés and restaurants with outside tables (not inside) and a large bucket of fresh dog water is nearly always provided for canine visitors. Don't be surprised if your waiter or other customers give your dog tid-bits, however improbable, without asking – this seems to be a conversation opener. Jem gained a passion for mussels and garlic bread in Sainte Cécile because I was too slow to remember that 'allergy' is the same in French as in English. The actual allergy was mine to garlic dogbreath, but if your dog has a sensitive digestion the results of this random treating can be catastrophic. This brings us on to dog poo. The picking-up rules are the same as in the UK but the supply of free bags is marvellous, especially at the seaside resorts. If you find yourself in the otherwise dog-unfriendly resort of Le Touquet, the free bags from the dispensers on the promenade are delightfully chic.

1

Les Hemmes de Marck

Before or after a ferry crossing this enormous sandy beach is a great place to take in fresh air and sea breezes. Even at the height of summer it's rarely busy, and children and dogs can run safely for miles.

Getting there

GPS: 50° 59' 12.8394'' N 1° 57' 43.38'' E
Distance from Calais: 9 km

From Calais Ferry Port
Follow the exit road to leave the ferry port and then turn right at the roundabout signed Oye-Plage, Marck. Drive over a level crossing and take the 2nd turning to the left onto Route de Gravelines (the sign says no left turn, but this is only for vehicles over 3.5 T). Follow this road for 4.8 km and, just when you're about to leave Le Fort Vert, turn left signed Les Hemmes de Marck. Carry on for 1.9 km, enter Les Hemmes de Marck and turn left just after a right turn to Oye Plage and a 45 km/hr speed limit sign. At the turning there is a small street sign for Chemin de la Digue. Follow this road as it bends right and turn left to reach the free parking at the beach.

From Eurotunnel Terminal
Exit the Eurotunnel terminal and bear right at the fork to join the A16, signed Calais, Lille, Reims, Paris. Leave the A16 at junction 48 signed for Marck-Ouest. Turn left, this is the D247 Rue Pascal. Go through one roundabout. At the second roundabout take exit 2,

D248, Avenue de Verdun. After 2 km turn right onto the D119 and after nearly 2 km turn left onto the D119E1, Rue des Islandais. Carry on for 1 km and then turn right, Rue Robelin, and after 150m bear left to stay on Rue Robelin. This becomes the coast road, Chemin de la Digue. Follow this road when it bends right and turn left to reach the free parking at the beach.

Walk

When the tide is out you'll find mile after mile of sandy beach, definitely a space for ball games and high octane rushing around.

At high tide the beach disappears, and a signed coastal path leads eastwards through the dunes above the high tide mark. After several miles you'll reach a bird reserve at Oye Plage and at migration time it's well worth taking binoculars with you to spot some of the thousands of birds taking a breather before heading north or south on their journey. It's possible to walk as far as the outskirts of Gravelines if you have several hours to spare.

Terrain: flat walking on or alongside the beach on soft sand and dunes.

Local info

Free parking. Campervan access.

Small outdoor café and WCs at a campsite on the track to the beach when open in summer. Campsite (www.les-palominos.com) accepts touring tents and campervans.

Nearest fuel station: 24/7 fuel at Esso Nord, 361 Ave Antoine de St-Exupery, Calais.

Nearest vet: Clinique Vétérinaire Saint Antoine, 127 Rue Pascal, 62730 Marck. Tel: 03 21 46 53 53 (on the D131 towards Calais).

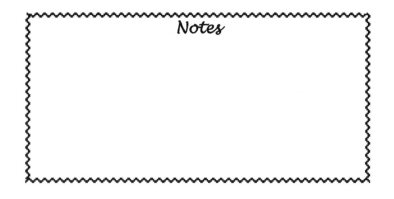

Notes

2

Forest of Éperlecques and Blockhaus d'Éperlecques

The Forest of Éperlecques covers a vast area and it would take a lot of walking to exhaust the many trails here.

Just a short way from the forest car park is the entrance to the extraordinary (and dog-friendly) outdoor museum of the Bunker of Éperlecques. During World War Two conscripts and prisoners were forced to build a mammoth facility intended to launch powerful V-2 rockets across the channel towards London. Fortunately the site didn't become operational, thanks to some sturdy sabotage work by the workforce. Today it's a sombre but fascinating place and of all the many military installations in the region now on show as 'heritage sites' on the tourist trail, we rated the information and visitor facilities here highly.

Getting there

GPS: 50° 49' 36.768'' N 2° 10' 55.4664'' E
Distance from Calais: 35.5 km

From Calais Ferry Port
Exit the ferry terminal and follow the signs for the A26, Paris, Reims. After 7 km, keep to the left hand lane, following signs for St Omer, Arras, Reims, Paris to join the A26.

From Eurotunnel Terminal
Exit the Eurotunnel terminal and bear right at the fork to join the A16, signed Calais, Lille, Reims, Paris. At junction 47, take the exit to join the A26 signed St Omer, Arras, Reims, Paris.

Both routes
Leave the A26 at junction 2 and take the D217, Éperlecques, Blockhaus d'Éperlecques. Turn right signed D943, St Omer, Blockhaus d'Éperlecques. Turn left signed D221, Bayenghem, Blockhaus d'Éperlecques. Continue straight ahead, driving through Le Mont, then pass the Château de Ganspette Campsite and turn left signed Blockhaus d'Éperlecques. Continue to reach the car parks, both are on the left and the forest car park is 50m before the entrance to the museum.

Walk

An information board in the car park gives an overview of the forest trails and wildlife you may be able to spot.

The trails aren't very clearly marked, but a pattern of 20 minutes heading rightwards, 20 minutes leftwards, and a final 20 minutes left again gave us a fabulous hour of circular walking. Dogs and children will adore the chance to hurtle around the woodland, while weary drivers may opt for the chance for a snooze under a tree in this tranquil and inviting woodland.

Paths are a mixture of clear forest tracks and footpaths.

Local info

Forest car park: cars only, free.

Blockhaus Museum car park: free, with zoned campervan and caravan parking.

Blockhaus museum: entry charge. Wheelchair access to museum, largely firm paths and concrete.

Refreshments: small selection of snacks, chocolate bars and hot/cold drinks at museum.

WC: inside museum.

Nearest supermarkets: Vival and Carrefour supermarkets in Watten.

Fuel: Carrefour supermarket on the D207, Rue de bleue Maison.

Tourist Information office: 12, rue de Dunkerque, Watten.

Nearest vet: Dr Jean Paulus, 21 Rue de bleue Maison, Éperlecques (at the D207/D300 junction). Tel: 03 21 88 46 00.

3
St Omer

On first arrival in St Omer you might think you've somehow strayed into Belgium. The centre of this pretty market town has a definite Flemish feel, the tall buildings with their high sloping roofs and window boxes stuffed with bright red flowers, and any number of beer bars spilling out onto broad pavements. St Omer is famous for its locally brewed beer.

With a dog-friendly budget hotel in the centre of the old town, a walk on the doorstep and shops to meet all needs, St Omer is a popular place to stay before or after a channel crossing.

Getting there

GPS: 50° 44' 52.5546'' N 2° 14' 57.8466'' E
Distance from Calais: 47 km

From Calais Ferry Port
Exit the ferry terminal and follow the signs for the A26, Paris, Reims. After 7 km, keep to the left hand lane, following the signs for St Omer, Arras, Reims, Paris to join the A26.

From Eurotunnel Terminal
Exit the Eurotunnel terminal and bear right at the fork to join the A16, signed Calais, Lille, Reims, Paris. At junction 47, take the exit to join the A26 signed St Omer, Arras, Reims, Paris.

Both routes
Leave the A26 at junction 3 and, after the péage, take exit 2 at the roundabout signed Setques, Wizernes, D342. After 1 km, turn left signed Wisques,

Longuenesse, D208E1 and carry straight on for 6.5 km. At the roundabout, take exit 3 signed St Omer. Keep straight on for 1 km and at a crossroads turn left signed St Martin au L, Centre Ville. Turn left at the roundabout to enter the car park.

Walk

The high walls of the park are all that's left of the historic ramparts of the medieval town, beefed up by Louis XIV in his successful campaign to wrest St Omer from Spanish control and annex the town to France in 1677. The walls are still impressively huge and were designed by Vauban, an extraordinarily energetic engineer who was responsible for over 300 fortifications throughout France.

To get into the 20 acre park, walk back to the main road from the parking space and turn left. Walk about 25 meters to the gate, and the path here will lead you into the formal gardens. Cut across these to the far right hand corner, and then you'll be on a firm path and into woodland. Dogs can be off-lead here.

A comfortable circuit around the park will take just under an hour. If you head towards the centre, look out for a small domestic animal zoo, with a collection of sociable goats, deer and poultry. Two popular play areas for young and older children are close to the zoo.

There's no fixed route here – the park is just the right size for a gentle amble without worrying about getting lost. Dogs should be on leads in the formal garden and on the circular jogging/cycle track, otherwise off-lead is fine.

Terrain: hard-surfaced paths suitable for wheelchairs/ buggies.

Local info

Free parking in the small car park by the Jardin Publiques. Campervan access. Also on-street metered parking in the town.

Refreshments: plenty of restaurants, bars and cafés near the central square. Large supermarkets (Carrefour, Lidl) in the Centre Commerciale (off the D928). Also artisan shops in the old town for stylish clothes and shoes, books and groceries.

WC: public conveniences opposite entrance to Jardin Publiques.

Fuel: Carrefour supermarket, on the D928 entering the town.

Tourist Information Office: 4, Rue du Lion d'Or, Saint Omer.

Nearest vet: Clinique Vétérinaire Sainte Marguerite, 20 Rue Faidherbe, Saint Omer. Tel: 03 21 98 67 90.

Market day is Wednesday morning.

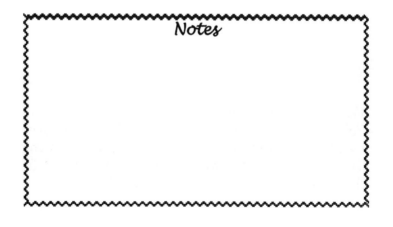

Notes

4

Forest of Guînes

The Forest of Guînes is famous for 'Blanchard's Column'. This marks the place where French aeronaut Jean-Pierre Blanchard and his American co-adventurer Dr Jeffries touched down on the first ever successful channel crossing by hot air balloon in 1785.

Train-spotters will also relish the sight of Eurostar trains passing under the bridge just before the car park.

The museum in Guînes village features events from the time of the Vikings up to the historic meeting between Henry VIII (England) and Francis I (France) in 1520 on the Field of the Cloth of Gold, an occasion for both kings to show off their wealth and status in grand style. Children can enjoy the museum's dressing-up box and lots of hands-on games here.

Getting there

GPS: 50° 50' 37.536'' N 1° 51' 59.148'' E
Distance from Calais: 25km

From Calais Ferry Port
Exit the ferry terminal and follow the signs for the A26, Paris, Reims. After 7 km, keep to the left hand lane, following the signs for St Omer, Arras, Reims, Paris to join the A26. Leave the A16 at junction 43 and, at the roundabout, take exit 3 signed Fréthun, Coulogne, Guînes, D304.

From Eurotunnel Terminal
Exit the Eurotunnel terminal and bear right at the fork to join the A16, signed Calais, Lille, Reims, Paris.

Leave the A16 at junction 43 and, at the roundabout, take exit 1 signed Fréthun, Coulogne, Guînes, D304.

Both routes
At the next roundabout, take exit 2, signed Fréthun, Coquelles, Guînes, D304. Carry straight on for 2 km, carrying straight on at one roundabout, and at the following roundabout take exit 2 signed Hames-Boucres, Guînes, D305. Carry straight on for another 4 km and at the next roundabout take exit 1 signed Guînes, Ardres, D127. Enter Guînes and continue along the road (which changes its number to D215E4) to the roundabout. Take exit 2 signed A16 Boulogne, and continue to a T-junction. Turn left signed Ardres, St Omer, D231 and take the 1st right turn, signed La Colonne Blanchard. Follow this lane for 2.5 km and, shortly after crossing the railway line, the parking area will be on the left hand side by the picnic tables.

Walk

From the car park a number of signed paths lead into the forest and a 3km circular route is marked with yellow bars painted onto the trees.

If you're not feeling energetic, it's a great place to enjoy a picnic under the shade of the trees and let Fido snuffle happily in the leaves. The paths are clear and very easy to follow.

To visit the exact site of the famous Cloth of Gold event it's now a field on the D231 (GPS: 50° 51' 8.2794" N 1° 55' 22.44" E). A small plaque marks the spot, and children at KS2 may be interested.

Local info

At forest: free parking. Campervan access. Picnic tables.

In Guînes: Metered on-street parking. Intermarché supermarket with fuel on the D231; Carrefour supermarket with 24hr fuel on D231 direction Ardres.

Museum: Tour la Horloge, Rue de Chateau, Guînes. Tel: 03 2119 5900. Opening hours vary.

Nearest vet: Cabinet Vétérinaire du Marais, 20 route Guînes, Hames Boucres (4.5km from Guînes). Tel: 03 21 85 18 50.

Market day: Friday morning.

5

Forest of Tournehem

The leafy glades of the Forest of Tournehem give welcome shade to walkers in summer and form a very effective natural umbrella on wet days.

The tiny chapel and the quietness of the forest make you feel as if you've discovered a truly secret place.

Getting there

GPS: 50° 45' 59.9594'' N 2° 2' 39.152'' E
Distance from Calais: 33.7 km

From Calais Ferry Port
Exit the ferry terminal and follow the signs for the A26, Paris, Reims. After 7 km, keep to the left hand lane, following the signs for St Omer, Arras, Reims, Paris to join the A26.

From Eurotunnel Terminal
Exit the Eurotunnel terminal and bear right at the fork to join the A16, signed Calais, Lille, Reims, Paris. At junction 47 take the exit to join the A26 signed St Omer, Arras, Reims, Paris.

Both routes
Leave the A26 at junction 2 and at the junction turn left signed Tournehem, Licques, D217. Enter Tournehem and continue to a T-junction. Turn right, signed Bonningues A, Licques, D217. Keep straight on for 3 km to enter Bonningues les Ardres and turn left signed Quercamps, Lumbres, D225. As the road goes uphill turn left just before a zig-zag bend onto a forest lane.

You'll see bright red and white bollards at the turning point. Continue on this lane to the car park.

Walk

A hard surface track leads straight into the woodland from the parking space. This is suitable for wheelchairs. Look out for the small forest church with votive offerings close to the car park. You can peer in through the grille on the side.

As well as the track you'll find any number of appealing grassy paths leading through groves of beech and hazel trees. In autumn locals come to gather nuts and go at it with fierce concentration. Otherwise the woodland is pretty much people-free, with an amazing high volume soundtrack of birdsong.

There isn't a fixed route, and the forest is so immense that you can visit time and again and not repeat your route. Allow at least 60 minutes for your walk.

Local info

Free parking. Campervan access.

Refreshments: Tournehem village: boulangerie on Rue Gen de Gaulle, Cocci market general stores for picnic supplies, and the Café de la Mairie in the centre.

Nearest fuel: 3 pumps at Bal Parc Autos, Rue de vieux Château. Opening hours vary.

Nearest vet: Groupe Vétérinaire, 11 Place Jean Jaurès, Lumbres. Tel: 03 21 39 60 19.

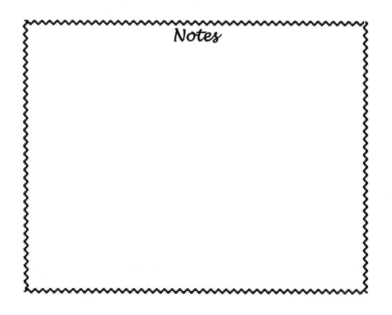

Notes

6

Cap Blanc Nez

This is so close to Dover you can almost touch the white cliffs across the water, and it's a popular place to find visitors gazing across to the fields of Kent.

An obelisk perched on the point commemorates the heroic work of the World War 1 'Dover Patrol' which somehow managed to keep the channel free of enemy

U-boats. A viewing platform has some informative panels about the history, and a telescope.

Getting there

GPS: 50° 55' 26.76'' N 1° 42' 59.004'' E
Distance from Calais: 23.5 km

From Calais Ferry Port
Exit the ferry terminal and follow the signs for the A26, Paris, Reims. After 7 km, keep to the right hand lane, following the signs for Tunnel Sous la Manche, Boulogne to join the A16.

From Eurotunnel Terminal
Exit the Eurotunnel terminal and bear left at the fork to join the A16, signed Boulogne, Rouen.

Both routes
Leave the A16 at junction 40 and follow the signs for Cap Blanc Nez, D215. The route to Cap Blanc Nez is fully signed.

Walk

The long distance coastal path (GR120) is clearly signposted between the car park and the obelisk. Turning left (west) is the better option for dog owners as the path stays well away from the road and gives dogs more scampering space. As soon as you leave the obelisk behind the prevailing breeze drops and you'll soon have the path to yourself as most visitors just orbit the viewing platform and then head back to their cars.

The route here is a linear walk on the coast path. As a rough guide to distance, after passing 'le Petit Blanc Nez' you'll be a quarter of the way to the sandy beach of Wissant. The town itself is further on, past the far end of the beach.

The hard surface path to the viewing platform is wheelchair accessible, as is the start of the coastal path.

Local info

Free parking. Campervan access.

Refreshments: Les Falaises café and restaurant, 18 Rue de la Mer, Escalles is on the way to the car park, open year round.

Fuel: none nearby.

Tourist Information Office: Place de la Mairie, Wissant.

Nearest vet: Clinique Vétérinaire Des Deux Caps, 9 Avenue Ferber, Marquise. Tel: 08 99 10 18 35 (8km from Cap Blanc Nez car park).

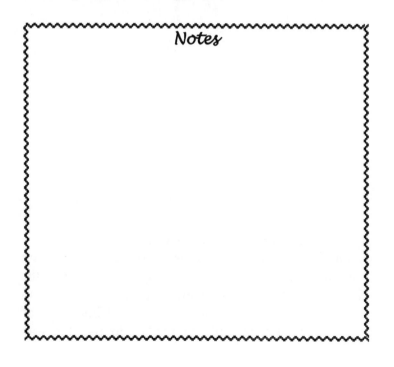

Notes

7

Wissant Beach

If you like quirky historical facts, Wissant deserves a moment of your time. It used to be an important harbour for cross-channel voyages, including the Romans starting one of their invasions of Britain in 55BCE. The story goes that Henry III of England was once stranded here with no readies to pay his way home. The same Henry later caused mayhem in the port by ordering the embarkation of a fully-grown elephant onto a wooden boat. Somehow the elephant survived its channel crossing and became a popular attraction in 13th century London. Roll on 800 years, and workers at a gravel quarry just west of Wissant dug up a complete mammoth skeleton, tusks and all.

Getting there

GPS: 50° 53' 15" N 1° 39' 40" E
Distance from Calais: 29.2 km

From Calais Ferry Port
Exit the ferry terminal and follow the signs for the A26, Paris, Reims. After 7 km, keep to the right hand lane, following the signs for Tunnel Sous la Manche, Boulogne to join the A16.

From Eurotunnel Terminal
Exit the Eurotunnel terminal and bear left at the fork to join the A16, signed Boulogne, Rouen.

Both routes
Leave the A16 at junction 38 and, at the T-junction, turn left signed St Inglevert, Wissant, Cap Gris Nez,

D244E1. At the roundabout, take exit 1 signed Wissant, D244. After 5.5 km, turn left at the T-junction, signed A16 (Boulogne), Wissant, D940 and continue to enter Wissant. Turn right, signed Wissant-Centre, Office du Tourisme and follow the road round to the right. Immediately after passing a church, turn left. Turn right at the T-junction and drive down the narrow lane marked with a one-way arrow. Follow this lane for 300m to reach the sea. The beach to the right is the most spacious.

Walk

The central town beach has dog restrictions in summer, so the place to head for is just around the headland to the east of the town. Here you'll find a huge sandy beach with deep rockpools, excellent for paddling and crab spotting. An old pill box lies in the middle of the beach, nearly a century of tidal battering has given it a significant tilt and colonies of small crustaceans have now moved in.

At high tide the beach can disappear entirely, but the dunes behind the beach stretch for miles and give protection from the generally keen prevailing breeze. The GR120 coastal path runs behind the dunes.

Local info

Free parking on the sea front east of the town. Campervan access.

Small local shops for picnic supplies and a Spar supermarket on the east side. Cafés and bars with dog-friendly outside tables and larger shops in the town centre.

Fuel: TOTAL, Avenue Ferber, Marquise (on D241).

Tourist Information Office: Place de la Mairie, Wissant.

Nearest vet: Clinique Vétérinaire des Deux Caps, 9 Avenue Ferber, Marquise. Tel: 03 21 92 89 12 (8.5km from Wissant on D241).

Notes

8

Cap Gris Nez

Cap Gris Nez is one of the closest points in France to the Kent coast and on a clear day you can easily see the white cliffs of Dover. Because France and England are so close here, the strategic importance of the cape over the centuries has been huge. Henry VIII had a fortress built on the north side of the cliff here in the 16th

century (when England owned quite a bit of northern France) and its earthworks can still be seen, although one side has now fallen into the sea.

Straight ahead and out to sea is the official point where the Channel and the North Sea meet.

Getting there

GPS: 50° 52' 9.1194'' N 1° 35' 10.896'' E
Distance from Calais: 39.4 km

From Calais Ferry Port
Exit the ferry terminal and follow the signs for the A26, Paris, Reims. After 7 km, keep to the right hand lane, following signs for Tunnel Sous la Manche, Boulogne to join the A16.

From Eurotunnel Terminal
Exit the Eurotunnel terminal and bear left at the fork to join the A16, signed Boulogne, Rouen.

Both routes
Leave the A16 at junction 36 and turn right at the T-junction, signed Bazinghen, Ambleteuse, D191. At the roundabout, take exit 2, signed Bazinghen, Cap Gris-

Nez, D191. After 2.5 km, turn right signed Audinghen, Cap Gris Nez, D191 and keep straight on for 7 km, carrying straight on at one roundabout. The road leads straight to the car park at Cap Gris Nez.

Walk

Most visitors to Cap Gris Nez just plod from the enormous car park to the viewing platform and then back to their vehicles. This is possibly the least attractive part of the walk and certainly the most windy section. And dogs must be on-lead here.

Instead, head towards the lighthouse but then bear either left or right on the waymarked GR120 coastal footpath and within minutes the prevailing wind calms and most of the other visitors will be left behind. Dogs can be off-lead on the coast path.

Turning right (east) will take you through Wissant and on towards Cap Blanc Nez, and a left turn (west) will take you first through the village of Audresselles and Ambleteuse after that. Both are good walks, and worth doing. Dogs should be on leads over part of the beach at Audresselles, especially when the black-headed seals are raising pups. There are signs.

Walk 2

Bois d'Haringzelles

If you're here on a grey misty day when a coast walk has little to attract, the nearby Bois d'Haringzelles makes a good alternative. This is a small wood, planted during World War 2 by the Germans to prevent a military installation from being spotted from the sea. It's a quiet and rather sombre place as the concrete bunker has been left in place. The domesticity of the soldiers' bread ovens seems bizarre when seen in the context of the gun emplacements above.

GPS co-ords for the Bois d'Haringzelles are: 50° 50' 21.5594" N 1° 35' 53.3" E. There's a small free car park. Height restriction of 2.1m but campervans can easily park on the track by the car park entrance. A military museum can also be visited a little further along the track.

Local info

Cap Gris Nez. Free car park. Height restriction 2.1m. No WCs at the car park.

In Audinghen: local shops, café and bars.

Fuel: Opel fuel 5km away on the D940.

Nearest vet: Clinique Vétérinaire des Deux Caps, 9 Avenue Ferber, 62250 Marquise (on D241). Tel: 03 21 92 89 12.

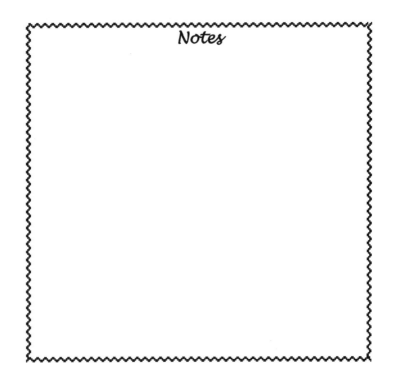

Notes

9

Forest of Desvres

Easily reached from Boulogne, the market town of
Desvres is worth a visit before or after a walk in the
forest. The town has been a centre for the design and
production of ceramics for hundreds of years and
there's a small ceramics museum (no dogs). The

ceramics shop near the museum is a great place to find unusual and authentic souvenirs of your visit.

Getting there

GPS: 50° 41' 12'' N 1° 49' 40'' E (forest)
Distance from Calais: 61.4 km

From Calais Ferry Port
Exit the ferry terminal and follow signs for the A26, Paris, Reims. After 7 km, keep to the right hand lane, following signs for Tunnel Sous la Manche, Boulogne to join the A16.

From Eurotunnel Terminal
Exit the Eurotunnel terminal and bear left at the fork to join the A16, signed Boulogne, Rouen.

Both routes
Leave the A16 at junction 31 and at the roundabout, take exit 2 signed Tunnel, Calais, Desvres, N42. Continue on the dual carriageway for 11.5 km (carrying straight on at one roundabout) and take the exit for Desvres, Le Wast, D127. At the roundabout, take exit 1 signed Alincthun, Desvres, D127. After 400m, turn left signed Alincthun, Desvres, D127. Keep ahead on this

road for 6.5 km to enter the forest. Park at the beginning of the forest track on the right (without blocking vehicle access).

Walk

The forest is vast, and offers plenty of space for a very long walk indeed.

The central track has a firm surface and is easy to follow, and will keep your feet clean and dry on wet days too. Grassy paths lead off into shady glades and dogs will find the scent of the local wildlife irresistible.

Local info

At the forest: free parking and campervan access.

In Desvres: free parking and campervan access. On market days (Tuesdays) park in the ceramics museum car park.

Refreshments: pâtisserie, boulangerie and cafés in Desvres.

Fuel: Esso Express, Route Boulogne, Longfosse (3km from Desvres on D204).

Tourist Information Office: 41 rue Potiers, Desvres.

Nearest vet: Clinique Vétérinaire, 16 rue Château, Desvres. Tel: 03 21 83 79 30.

Market day is Tuesday.

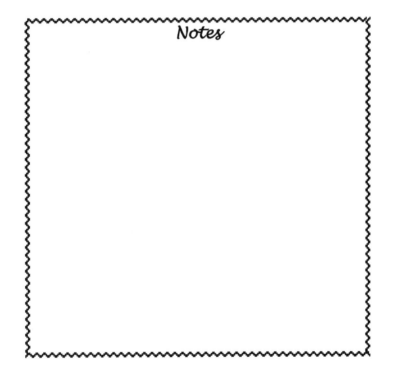

Notes

10

Forest of Boulogne

Once a royal hunting preserve, today the forest of Boulogne is over 2,000 hectares of fabulously lush greenery. In summer the tree canopy is cooling, while in wet weather you're protected from the rain.

Getting there

GPS: 50° 41' 9.9954'' N 1° 43' 49.5474'' E
Distance from Calais: 51km

From Calais Ferry Port
Exit the ferry terminal and follow the signs for the A26, Paris, Reims. After 7 km, keep to the right hand lane, following the signs for Tunnel Sous la Manche, Boulogne to join the A16.

From Eurotunnel Terminal
Exit the Eurotunnel terminal and bear left at the fork to join the A16, signed Boulogne, Rouen.

Both routes
Leave the A16 at junction 31 and at the roundabout take exit 2 signed Tunnel, Calais, N42. After 350m, take exit 1 at the next roundabout signed St Martin-B, Baincthun. This road runs alongside the A16 for 850m then, at the T-junction, turn left signed Baincthun, Desvres, D341. Stay on the D341 to enter the Forêt Dominale de Boulogne. Continue ahead on the D341 through Mont Lambert, Baincthun and Fort Mahon. 2 km after leaving Fort Mahon, the road swings round to the left. After rounding this bend, park in the pull in/forestry gate on the left hand side.

Walk

There are several pull-in places to start your walk, we chose one by 'Tree 87' as this is on the well-signed Tour du Boulonnais footpath, marked with red and yellow horizontal flashes painted onto the trees. It's also a bridlepath so horses are a possibility.

This is a linear walk on part of the long distance path, and offers miles of walking. Don't forget to turn around at your half-way point.

Local info

Free parking. Campervan access for small vans.

Nearest fuel: Esso Express, Route Boulogne, Longfosse (on D204).

Nearest vets: Clinique Vétérinaire les Margats, 14 Avenue Charles de Gaulle, Boulogne-sur-Mer. Tel. 03 21 83 13 81

Clinique Vétérinaire, 16 rue Château, Desvres. Tel: 03 21 83 79 30.

11
Equihen Plage

No dog restrictions on this lovely sandy beach, and it's plenty big enough to get Fido's little legs tired out. We were fascinated by the air-sailing school and watching the novices get airborne must be a popular pastime for locals. The number of wooden benches in sheltered nooks is the giveaway. Look out for the unusual accommodation at the campsite – upturned boats that look great and celebrate the local fishing tradition.

Getting there

GPS: 50° 40' 4.44" N 1° 34' 13.5474" E
Distance from Calais: 59.4 km

From Calais Ferry Port
Exit the ferry terminal and follow the signs for the A26, Paris, Reims. After 7 km, keep to the right hand lane, following the signs for Tunnel Sous la Manche, Boulogne to join the A16.

From Eurotunnel Terminal
Exit the Eurotunnel terminal and bear left at the fork to join the A16, signed Boulogne, Rouen.

Both routes
Leave the A16 at junction 28 and, at the roundabout, take exit 1 signed Boulogne, D901. Carry straight on at the next roundabout. At the next roundabout, take exit 2 signed Berck, Le Touquet, D940. After 0.5 km take the very hard right turn at the lights, signed Arena Ecault, and 150m later turn left following the blue sign for Complexes Sportifs. Take the 1st right turn and continue straight to a T-junction. Turn left, signed Equihen Plage, D235, and drive into the village of Ecault. In the village, turn right signed Equihen Plage, D119.

Continue ahead for 1.8 km and follow the sign for Equihen Plage at the next roundabout. Enter Equihen Plage and take exit 2 at the roundabout, signed Plage. Continue straight on to reach the car park.

Walk

The long sandy beach goes on for miles, and is ideal for a family walk and swim combo. During French school holidays the beach can get crowded but you only have to walk for 10 minutes to get away from the deckchairs.

Pick up picnic supplies on your way down to the beach. It's a long uphill walk to the shops on the road from the beach.

Local info

Free parking. Campervan access in upper car park, 2.1m height restriction at the lower car park. WCs and disabled. Ramp access to beach suitable for wheelchairs.

Local shops in Equihen town: patisserie, boulangerie, small general stores and pharmacy. Cafés, seasonal opening. Camping: La Falaise, opposite the upper car park.

Fuel: Carrefour supermarket, rue d'Acacias, Outreau (2km away, North on D119).

Nearest vet: Clinique Vétérinaire Opal, 62 Boulevard Gén de Gaulle, Portel (on the D236 2.75km from Equihen). Tel: 03 21 33 35 33.

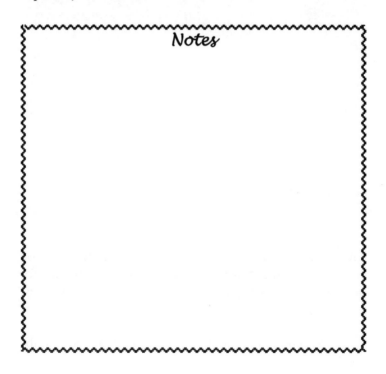

Notes

12

Forest of Ecault

The maritime Forest of Ecault is well-used by local dog walkers, and those we met were very keen to stop for doggie chats and to tell us how marvellous their forest is for walking.

If you're here in autumn, take a bag with you and join the locals in a fabulous forage for berries, nuts and mushrooms.

Getting there

GPS: 50° 39' 19.0794'' N 1° 36' 32.0394'' E
Distance from Calais: 54.5 km

From Calais Ferry Port
Exit the ferry terminal and follow the signs for the A26,
Paris, Reims. After 7 km, keep to the right hand lane,
following the signs for Tunnel Sous la Manche,
Boulogne to join the A16.

From Eurotunnel Terminal
Exit the Eurotunnel terminal and bear left at the fork to
join the A16, signed Boulogne, Rouen.

Both routes
Leave the A16 at junction 29 and at the roundabout, take
exit 1 signed Boulogne-Centre, N1. At the next
roundabout, take exit 2 signed Outreau, Le Portel, N1.
Keep in the left hand lane and at the next roundabout,
take exit 3 signed Outreau-Manihen, D901E3. At the
next roundabout, take exit 2 signed Outreau Centre,
Manihen, D52E2. Immediately after the level crossing,
turn left at a T-junction signed Manihen. Continue for
1.5 km then turn right signed Equihen-Plage, Condette,
Hardelot, D235, and continue ahead to enter Ecault. At
the T-junction bear left, signed Condette, Hardelot, D119

and keep straight on for 1.5 km. Turn right at the brown sign for Forêt Dominale d'Ecault to reach the car park.

Walk

There are lots of small paths that meander away from a central forest track, so although there isn't a signed route it's easy to strike off into the trees and still keep your bearings.

This is a great place for a family nature trail, with all sorts of shrubs and wildflowers to identify and possibly eat, as well as a thriving population of small furry animals for kids to spot (and dogs to chase). The central track is firm and buggy/wheelchair accessible.

Local info

Free parking. Campervan access. Picnic tables.

In Condette: Carrefour supermarket, patisserie, boulangerie, cafés and fuel.

Nearest vet: Clinique Vétérinaire Cent Dunes, No. 50 on the D940, Condette. Tel: 03 21 87 61 87; 03 21 83 02 18.

13

Hardelot Plage

Loosely attached to the small town of Neufchâtel-Hardelot this seaside resort has something of an English feel to it. You'll notice this in the distinctly un-Gallic one-way system to reach the beach. The resort was first developed by a Brit, Sir John Whitely, in the 1900s. His design was largely blown up during World War 2 so what you see today is all relatively modern, and impeccably clean and tidy.

Getting there

GPS: 50° 38' 21.84'' N 1° 34' 37.7754'' E
Distance from Calais: 65.4 km

From Calais Ferry Port
Exit the ferry terminal and follow the signs for the A26,
Paris, Reims. After 7 km, keep to the right hand lane,
following the signs for Tunnel Sous la Manche,
Boulogne to join the A16.

From Eurotunnel Terminal
Exit the Eurotunnel terminal and bear left at the fork to
join the A16, signed Boulogne, Rouen.

Both routes
Leave the A16 at junction 27 and at the roundabout take
exit 1 signed Ste Cécile, Desvres, D308. At the next
roundabout, take exit 1 signed Boulogne, Neufchâtel-
Hardelot, D940. Almost immediately, get into the left
hand lane and turn left for Château Hardelot. Continue
ahead for 2 km, then turn left signed Hardelot – La
Plage. At the next roundabout, take exit 2 signed La
Plage. Carry straight on to the point where there are two
right turns close together (by a car parking area and the
way ahead blocked by houses). Take the 2nd of these

right turns, then take the 1st left turn. Continue straight on to reach the sea and turn right. Continue ahead, keeping the sea to your left, and park near the apartments.

Walk

Dogs are banned from the beach directly in front of the town in the summer, but the walk from the East (right-hand side) of the beach is a complete winner. It starts at the point where the promenade finishes and the dunes begin, and is a signed section of the GR120 coast path.

We walked along the beach to Equihen and back. It doesn't sound that exciting, but the opportunities for kids and dogs to race around the dunes and then across the sand and into the sea are limitless. And the sense of open space when the tide's out is fantastic: big views, big sea and big sky and hardly anyone around except other walkers. You'll have a happy, tired out family after a walk here for sure.

Local info

Limited free parking and campervan access at the East side of the sea front at Neufchâtel-Hardelot. Food stores, pharmacy, restaurants on Avenue de la Concorde on the approach to the beach.

Fuel: Carrefour market, Neufchâtel-Hardelot on the D113 on the edge of the 'old' town.

Nearest vet: Clinique Vétérinaire Cent Dunes, Number 50, on the D940, Condette. Tel: 03 21 87 61 87.

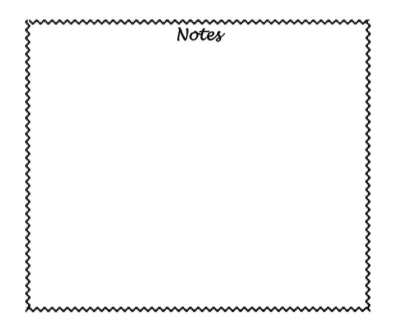

Notes

14
Sainte Cécile

Sainte Cécile is a popular summer resort with plenty going on in season. If you're juggling the needs of family, dog and friends then this is a good bet to keep everyone happy.

Getting there

GPS: 50° 34' 30'' N 1° 34' 39.576'' E
Distance from Calais: 65.8 km

From Calais Ferry Port
Exit the ferry terminal and follow the signs for the A26, Paris, Reims. After 7 km, keep to the right hand lane, following the signs for Tunnel Sous la Manche, Boulogne to join the A16.

From Eurotunnel Terminal
Exit the Eurotunnel terminal and bear left at the fork to join the A16, signed Boulogne, Rouen.

Both routes
Leave the A16 at junction 27. After the péage, take exit 1 at the roundabout, signed Ste Cécile, D308. At the next roundabout, take exit 2 signed Le Touquet, Ste Cécile, D940. Continue ahead on the D940 for 5 km, crossing one roundabout, and at the next roundabout take exit 1 signed Ste Cécile Plage. Continue straight on to reach the parking bays by the sea.

Walk

The Côte d'Opale is rightly famous for its massive sandy beaches, and Sainte Cécile is blessed with even more dog-friendly sand as it's on a corner where the river Canche meets the sea. The beach is divided into two parts. Dogs are banned from the beach directly in front of the town, but are free to romp on the sands to the left of the town. You'll still find a number of shops, cafés and ice-cream parlours on this side.

Turn left along the beach (with the sea ahead of you) and join the coastal path for a lovely long walk on the firm sand. If you walk far enough, the signed coast path turns inland and skirts the edge of the Bay of Canche Nature Reserve, and towards the small town of Camiers. This would be quite a hike, and a there-and-back on the beach is a safer option so that you can keep an eye on the tide.

This walk is best started as the tide starts to go out; and is not recommended when the tide is coming in because of the unpredictable combination of river mouth and fast incoming water by the nature reserve.

Local info

Free parking. Campervan access.

Refreshments: cafés with lots of outside seating on the sea front, dogs welcome at all outside tables. Shops and take-aways on the main street, some open in season only.

Fuel: TOTAL, Avenue Aéroport, Cucq.

Nearest vet: Clinique Vétérinaire de la Côte d'Opale 1288 Avenue Libération, Cucq. Tel: 03 21 94 02 56.

Market day: Monday and Thursday mornings in July and August.

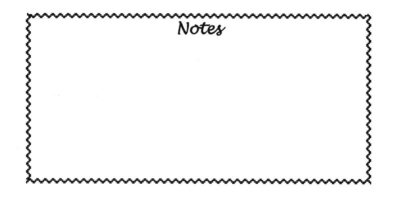

Notes

15

Robert du Rohart Nature reserve

A small but outstanding nature reserve near Camiers where a mix of peat bog and sand form a unique environment in which native, but now rare, dragonflies, frogs and birds can find sanctuary.

Getting there

GPS: 50° 34' 31'' N 1° 36' 21'' E
Distance from Calais: 64.1 km

From Calais Ferry Port
Exit the ferry terminal and follow the signs for the A26, Paris, Reims. After 7 km, keep to the right hand lane, following the signs for Tunnel Sous la Manche, Boulogne to join the A16.

From Eurotunnel Terminal
Exit the Eurotunnel terminal and bear left at the fork to join the A16, signed Boulogne, Rouen.

Both routes
Leave the A16 at junction 27. After the péage, take exit 1 at the roundabout, signed Ste Cécile, D308. At the next roundabout, take exit 2 signed Le Touquet, Ste Cécile, D940. Continue on the D940 for 5 km, cross one roundabout and at the next roundabout take exit 3 signed Camiers. After a 45 km/hr speed restriction sign, park in the lay-by on the right.

Walk

Visitors are welcome in this extraordinary 12 hectare nature reserve and a wooden walkway over the swamp takes you around on a short circular route. It's wheelchair and buggy-safe, and dogs are welcome as long as they don't leap into the water.

The reserve is part of a wider wildlife conservation project in the area and completely engrossing. Definitely a place to take your camera and binoculars, and to enjoy sightings of rare and delicate species of moths and amphibians.

Local info

Free parking. Campervan access.

Refreshments: local shops in Camiers, seaside cafés/restaurants in Ste Cécile.

Fuel: TOTAL, Avenue Aéroport, Cucq (6km).

Nearest vet: Dr Laurent Goube, 18 Boulevard Bigot Descelers, Etaples sur Mer. Tel: 03 21 94 67 01 (8km).

Market day Camiers: Monday morning.

Notes

16
Stella

The small resort of Stella tends to come to life only during sunny summer weekends. At other times you're likely to share this glorious sandy beach only with dog walkers.

There's near unlimited space for doggy dashing and splashing, and definitely a great place for family ball games and even 4-paws football. Even when the tide is fully in you'll still find a wide band of sand for a good leg-stretch in either direction.

Getting there

GPS: 50° 28' 52.32'' N 1° 34' 35.076'' E
Distance from Calais: 81.4 km

From Calais Ferry Port
Exit the ferry terminal and follow signs for the A26, Paris, Reims. After 7km, keep to the right hand lane, following the signs for Tunnel Sous la Manche, Boulogne to join the A16.

From Eurotunnel Terminal
Exit the Eurotunnel terminal and bear left at the fork to join the A16, signed Boulogne, Rouen.

Both routes
Leave the A16 at junction 26. After the péage continue ahead to the roundabout and take exit 1 signed Le Touquet, Etaples, D939. Continue straight on at the next roundabout, signed Le Touquet, Etaples Centre, D939 and bear left at the mini-roundabout, still following Le Touquet, Etaples Centre, D939. At the next roundabout, take exit 4 signed Le Touquet, Stella Plage, D939. Cross the river and at the next roundabout

take exit 3 signed Berck, Stella Plage, D940 (there is a McDonalds on this roundabout). Continue ahead for 1.5 km and then follow the road round to the right, still signed Berck, Stella Plage, D940. Go straight on for another 1.5 km, then turn right at the roundabout, signed Stella Plage, D144. Turn left at the next roundabout, signed Stella Plage, D144, follow the road as it bears round to the right and continue straight on to reach the parking area near the beach.

Walk

Jem gives this the paws-up for a doggie ideal beach. Swimming, running, chasing and rolling on kilometres of clean sand is off-lead delight with not a dog restriction in sight. You can walk across the sand to Le Touquet (generally not dog-friendly although you do find poo-bag dispensers on the promenade there with very chic, free bags) and the extensive dunes behind the beach are great for a snooze.

It's essential to keep an eye on the tide tables, you'll see the boards on all the Opal Coast beaches, so that you don't get stranded on a sand bar by the very fast incoming tide.

Local info

Free parking on the sea front, WCs, campervan access.

Refreshments: small restaurants with plenty of outside seating (covered on windy/wet days) and most have large buckets of water for dogs. Brasserie de la Plage open mid Jan to mid-November; L'Escale open all year. Supermarket on the D144 towards Cucq for fuel and picnic supplies.

Nearest vet: Clinique Vétérinaire de la Côte d'Opale, 1288 Avenue Libération, Cucq. Tel: 03 21 94 02 56.

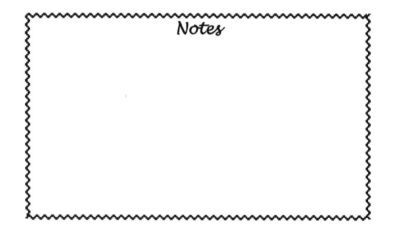

Notes

17
Montreuil-sur-Mer

Montreuil was once a thriving port town, but today several kilometres of dunes and marshes have cut off the harbour from the sea. So what we see today is a lovely example of a medieval walled city that escaped much of the battering of World War 2. It's known as the 'Carcassonne of the North' in France.

Fans of Les Misérables will know all about this medieval town as this is where the action at the beginning of the story takes place. In real life, Les Mis author Victor Hugo regularly stayed at the Hôtel de France for secret trysts with his mistress, and then based some of the book's characters on real people in the town.

Getting there

GPS: 50° 27' 57.2394'' N 1° 45' 37.6554'' E
Distance from Calais: 80.4 km

From Calais Ferry Port
Exit the ferry terminal and follow the signs for the A26, Paris, Reims. After 7 km, keep to the right hand lane, following the signs for Tunnel Sous la Manche, Boulogne to join the A16.

From Eurotunnel Terminal

Exit the Eurotunnel terminal and bear left at the fork to join the A16, signed Boulogne, Rouen.

Both routes
Leave the A16 at junction 26. After the péage turn left at the roundabout signed Arras, Montreuil, D939. Continue on the D939 for 7 km, then take exit 1 at the roundabout signed Abbeville, Montreuil, D901. After 1 km, turn right at the traffic lights, signed Montreuil Centre. Continue up a hill and turn right, signed Montreuil sur Mer Ville Haute. Pass through the archway and continue along the cobbled road as far as a small square. There is parking here. Alternatively, for disabled and limited general parking, turn right at the end of the square (there's a small sign for Château de Montreuil) and park in front of the tourist office. Parking is also available in the Charles de Gaulle car park or in the Market Square.

Walk

The walk here takes you around the city, following the line of the ancient ramparts. The first section was built in the 9th century when the town was a bustling sea port. After that, silt blocked access to the sea, medieval wars did for much of the castle towers and ramparts and, finally, plague decimated the population.

The circular walk around the ramparts starts from just past the Tourist Information Office and is well signed. The full route is quite long, but it's easy to start on the ramparts and then divert into the very attractive town for shopping and refreshments.

Local info

Free parking close to the Tourist Office. Shops, cafés and restaurants in the town centre.

Fuel: TOTAL, 43 Avenue du Général Leclerc (on approach to town from the A16) open Sundays.

Tourist Information office: 21 rue Carnot, Montreuil-sur-Mer.

Nearest vet: Drs Ollevier and Osset, 2 Avenue Gén Leclerc, Montreuil-sur-Mer. Tel: 03 21 06 22 03.

Market day: Saturday.

18
Berck-sur-Mer

The small town of Berck is active all through the year
and so you'll find plenty of open shops and cafés
whenever you go. The beach is enormous and hugely
popular with families and dog walkers. Berck prides
itself on family-friendliness, and the traditional carousel
at the sea front is a gem.

The best-selling true story of Jean Dominique Bauby, 'The Diving Bell and the Butterfly', was both written and filmed here. A kite festival with sand yachts and all sorts of wind-powered contraptions takes place every April.

Getting there

GPS: 50° 24' 11.5194'' N 1° 33' 27.3954'' E
Distance from Calais: 92.5 km

From Calais Ferry Port
Exit the ferry terminal and follow the signs for the A26, Paris, Reims. After 7 km, keep to the right hand lane, following the signs for Tunnel Sous la Manche, Boulogne to join the A16.

From Eurotunnel Terminal
Exit the Eurotunnel terminal and bear left at the fork to join the A16, signed Boulogne, Rouen.

Both routes
Leave the A16 at junction 25. After the péage, take exit 2 at the roundabout, signed Berck, D303. Continue straight ahead over the next 2 roundabouts, both signed Berck, D303, then at the next roundabout

take exit 1 signed Le Touquet, D940 (there is a McDonalds on this roundabout). Turn left at the next roundabout and continue ahead through the town of Berck to reach the beach. For the best dog walking, turn left on reaching the sea and continue to the parking area at the end.

Walk

Out of season all 14km of the beach here is open to dog walkers. In season (July and August) dogs are welcome on the promenade and also have access to the sandy beach from the west side, just after the easily spotted old maritime hospital building.

You can walk for miles here. Even when the tide is in there's a coastal path to follow around the headland. This path is hard-surfaced for quite a while, and easily manageable with buggies and wheelchairs.

Local info

Free parking and campervan access at sea front car parks.

Plenty of shops for picnic supplies, cafés and restaurants – most with big dog water bowls in summer.

Supermarket with fuel: Carrefour, Avenue de Verdun, Berck.

Tourist Information Office: 5 avenue Francis Tattegrain, Berck.

Nearest vet: Dr Xavier Dubois, 421 Rue de l' Impératrice, Berck-sur-Mer. Tel: 03 21 94 49 48.

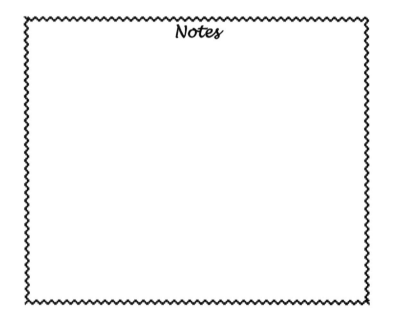

Notes

19

La Baie d'Authi Sud

A stunning expanse of sand flats held together by coastal plants and grasses.

Getting there

GPS: 50° 21' 18.72'' N 1° 34' 16.3194'' E
Distance from Calais: 101 km

From Calais Ferry Port
Exit the ferry terminal and follow the signs for the A26,
Paris, Reims. After 7 km, keep to the right hand lane,
following the signs for Tunnel Sous la Manche,
Boulogne to join the A16.

From Eurotunnel Terminal
Exit the Eurotunnel terminal and bear left at the fork to
join the A16, signed Boulogne, Rouen.

Both routes
Leave the A16 at junction 25. After the péage, take exit
2 at the roundabout, signed Berck, D303. Carry straight
on over the next roundabout then, soon after a level
crossing, turn left at the traffic lights, signed Verton
Centre, Quend, Fort-Mahon, D143. Drive through
Verton, continuing straight on at a roundabout in the
village centre, then drive straight through the village of
Waben. The road now passes a series of lakes. After
crossing the bridge over a river, turn right signed Fort-
Mahon, Baie d'Authie, D532. Continue into Fort-
Mahon-Plage and, at the T-junction, turn right.
Continue straight on for 1.5 km to reach the car park.

Walk

Allow several hours to get a feel for the dramatic beauty of this headland nature park. It's a stunning place for walks and no matter how many times you return the colours and shapes will always look different.

Pathways run in several directions across the sand and are easy to follow.

Be aware of the tide by checking the signs in the car park before you set out. The incoming tide can be dangerous.

Local info

Free parking and easy campervan access at La Baie d'Authi Sud car park.

In Fort Mahon: small shops for picnic supplies and pharmacy.

Fuel: Carrefour supermarket, 940 Avenue Verdun, Berck.

Tourist Information Office: 1000 Avenue Plage, Fort Mahon.

Nearest vet: Xavier Dubois, 421 Rue Impératrice, Berck (8km) Tel: 03 21 94 49 48.

20

Crécy Battlefield and Forest

A visit to Crécy wouldn't be complete without a small detour to experience at first hand a king's eye view of the famous battlefield where an outnumbered, but not out-classed, Anglo-Welsh army managed to rout the French in 1346. The site of the battle has been preserved, and the windmill commandeered by Edward

III as a royal grandstand is now rebuilt with useful interpretation boards for visitors.

Getting there

GPS for Battlefield: 50° 15' 22.356'' N 1° 53' 12.984'' E
GPS for Forest Walk: 50° 14' 15.057'' N 1° 51' 24.39'' E
Distance from Calais: 114 km

From Calais Ferry Port
Exit the ferry terminal and follow the signs for the A26, Paris, Reims. After 7 km, keep to the right hand lane, following the signs for Tunnel Sous la Manche, Boulogne to join the A16.

From Eurotunnel Terminal
Exit the Eurotunnel terminal and bear left at the fork to join the A16, signed Boulogne, Rouen.

Both routes
Leave the A16 at junction 25. After the péage, take exit 1 at the roundabout signed Arras, D303. After 750m take the 1st right turn (unsigned) and continue for 2 km to enter Wailly-Beaucamp. Turn right at the crossroads and continue ahead for the next 16 km. Take the right turn for Rue, Arry, Crécy-en-P, D938 then, at a T-junction, turn right signed Crécy-en-P, D938. Keep straight on to enter Crécy and take the right turn signed

Le Forêt, D111. Continue ahead to drive into the forest and park in the 1st parking area on the right hand side.

To reach the battlefield site, return to Crécy and turn right at the T-junction. Continue through the village centre until a signed left turn for 'Site du Champ de Bataille', D12. Then turn right signed 'Champs de B' and Wadicourt. Park in the signed parking area on the left hand side, almost immediately opposite the windmill-like lookout tower.

Forest of Crécy walk

Close to the town of Crécy-en-Ponthieu the forest stretches out for miles. Crécy forest is one of the largest forests in France.

From the parking pull-in you'll see a hard-surfaced forest track. This is ideal for buggies, kids on bikes and wheelchair users and it goes on for mile after mile. Smaller paths lead off the track and are great for exploring more of the forest, and trying to spot wildlife and interesting plants and toadstools. In season you may be lucky and find berries to snack on.

It's easy to forget the time here and wander through the forest for hours. Navigation is easy as long as you stay aware of your distance from the main track.

Local info

At the battlefield: Free parking, campervan access, WCs, picnic tables.

In Crécy-en-Ponthieu: free parking, campervan access, local shops for picnic supplies.

Market day: Monday

At Crécy forest: free parking, campervan access, no facilities.

Fuel: nearest stations are in Montrueil, Hesdin or Berck.

Nearest vet: Joel Serroyen, 2 Rue Croisie, Estrées-lès-Crécy (on D224b). Tel: 03 22 23 36 97.

Notes

Tiny Tick – Big Bite!

Whether you live in the countryside, town or city, going into fields, woodland, parks, or even your garden, can give ticks (blood-sucking parasites) the opportunity to bite you and your dog.

If you're thinking your dog is too clean to get ticks, think again! Ticks will happily feed on any person or animal that is clean, dirty, wet or dry.

If you're thinking your dog has never had ticks, think again! Many people think ticks are fat (like a baked bean) because they've seen them after several days of bloodsucking, when they stick out through the hair of a pet. Unfed, ticks can be flat and as tiny as a poppy seed (0.5mm). Recent research demonstrated that at least fifteen percent of dogs have ticks without their owner's knowledge.

Bad bugs!
Ticks aren't just a passing irritation. Their bites can result in uncomfortable skin reactions and septic abscesses, to the transmission of serious diseases. Preventing tick bites, and correctly removing any ticks

that are attached and feeding, is key to preserving your pet's health and your own.

The most common ticks in the UK to bite pets and people are the sheep tick and the hedgehog tick which, unlike their names suggest, happily feed on various animal species. They also transmit diseases such as Lyme disease (Borreliosis).

Lyme disease is prevalent throughout the UK, France, Germany, Scandinavia and other northern and central European countries. It causes inflammation to the joints, nervous system and heart, and affects people, dogs and horses in particular.

Although rarely reported in UK-resident dogs, Babesiosis (another tick-borne disease) can rapidly prove fatal and poses a significant threat to dogs living in, and visiting, other European countries.

A variety of tick-control products are available to protect pets against ticks. Monthly treatment is important to ensure the best possible protection. Ask your vet for advice and always read the manufacturers' instructions carefully before applying any product to avoid any adverse reactions.

Where your dog goes, you go…
Make sure you use a repellent too. Those containing DEET or lemon eucalyptus are particularly effective against ticks.

Do the 'tick check'!
The longer a tick feeds, the higher the risk of infection. Checking yourself and pets regularly for ticks allows you to find them before, or soon after, they begin feeding.

Correct tick removal reduces infection risk
Using fine-tipped tweezers, grasp the tick close to its mouth parts (where they are embedded in the skin). Steadily pull it outwards without jerking or twisting. Never squeeze the tick's body, burn, freeze, or smother it in substances such as petroleum jelly, spirits or oils. These methods are thought to induce back-flow of fluids from the tick which may contain disease-causing organisms. Tick removers are available from veterinary surgeries, pet shops, chemists and outdoor shops. Always follow the manufacturer's instructions.
For more information, visit www.bada-uk.org

Article provided by BADA, with thanks.

Other titles by Lezli Rees

Walking the Dog: walks for dogs and drivers near UK
motorway exits. RAC Publications.
ISBN 978-1-845841-02-7

For the latest news and more walks please visit
www.drivingwithdogs.co.uk

Lightning Source UK Ltd.
Milton Keynes UK
UKHW040626200319
339513UK00001B/6/P